Socialism and Liberation in the United States

PSL PUBLICATIONS

SAN FRANCISCO

Library of Congress Control Number: 2010937412
ISBN: 978-0-9841220-2-8
Printed in the United States
Cover photo: Bill Hackwell

Party for Socialism and Liberation

Editors

Andy McInerney, Ian Thompson

Staff

Meghann Adams, Joe Delaplaine, Anne Gamboni,
Saul Kanowitz, Susan Muysenburg, Keith Pavlik

PSL Publications

3181 Mission Street #13
San Francisco, CA 94110
(415) 821-6171
books@PSLweb.org
www.PSLweb.org

Socialism and Liberation in the United States

Foreword

THIS book is comprised of two documents written by the Party for Socialism and Liberation.

The first, "The Program of the Party for Socialism and Liberation," was adopted by the First Congress of the PSL in February 2010. It is a political program that outlines what a workers' government would do upon a revolutionary triumph in the United States.

The second, "Who We Are, What We Stand For" is the revised 2010 edition of a document approved and adopted by the PSL in January 2005, shortly after its founding. It includes the PSL's assessment of the current international and domestic situation and the need to build a revolutionary workers' party in the United States.

We hope you agree with the PSL's analysis and vision. If you do, we invite you to join us in the struggle for socialism. There is no better time than now to build a revolutionary party in the heartland of world imperialism. ☐

The Program of the Party for Socialism and Liberation

Part 1

The struggle for socialism

THE Party for Socialism and Liberation exists to carry out the struggle for socialism inside the United States, the center of world capitalism and imperialism. The PSL stands in solidarity with our sisters and brothers around the world who are resisting capitalist exploitation and imperialist domination.

The need for the socialist reorganization of society becomes more apparent and urgent with each passing day. While a tiny part of the population grows ever richer, tens of millions of workers here in the United States and billions of workers around the world sink deeper into poverty. Monumental advances in science and technology, which could have uplifted the many, instead have mainly enriched the few.

The great wealth of society is the product of both natural resources and the labor of working people. Yet, that wealth is increasingly the private property of those who produce nothing of value—the tiny class of capitalist owners. This irreconcilable conflict defines life for the vast majority of people in the world.

The development of capitalism—as already foreseen by Karl Marx and Frederick Engels in the mid-19th century—binds the world ever more closely together. Today, there is a vast and growing international working class, of which the U.S. working class is but one section.

The working class is defined by its relationship to the means of production and to those who own the means of production, the capitalist class. The working class, deprived of ownership of private property, must work for wages or salaries paid by those who own the means of production. The working class also includes the "army of the unemployed," those who are kept as a reserve labor force. This army of reserve labor has become a permanent feature in modern capitalist society.

3

While the working class is not a monolithic entity, it is united by its defining features: the lack of ownership of private property and the requirement to work for those who own private property, the capitalists, or for the capitalist government. The capitalists own the banks, corporations, factories, warehouses, retail outlets and major media. In a very real way, they control the lives of workers and the unemployed.

But the working class sets into motion the means of production, distribution and communication. It can shut down production and the capitalist economy as a whole. It is the vast majority of humanity and has vast potential power. It holds the ability to create a new society.

21ST CENTURY IMPERIALISM

As Marxists in the United States, our starting point is an assessment of the world situation, of the struggle between the classes on an international scale. Only by taking the international situation as the point of departure is it possible for our strategy and tactics to conform to the needs of the working class and oppressed peoples worldwide. Nowhere is this approach more critically important than in the United States, the most powerful imperialist country in the world today.

Twenty-first century capitalism in the United States and the other imperialist countries is monopoly capitalism, which is dominated by the giant banks and other institutions of finance capital. Because of their economies of scale, marketing muscle and deep financial pockets, huge monopolies have increasingly squeezed out independent small- and medium-sized businesses and farming operations. This has largely eliminated the so-called "free market."

At the same time, the ruthlessness of monopoly capitalism has greatly sharpened the contradictions inherent in the system. The growing tendency toward catastrophic crises, militarism and war has resulted in the monopolies becoming merged with the capitalist state and government. Big banks and corporations now dominate the global economy, oppressing entire nations and continents, as well as the working class as a class.

While Wall Street is the center of world finance capitalism, the Pentagon is the headquarters of a military machine that occupies many lands and has bases in more than 100 countries. The military is the enforcer and protector of U.S. capitalism and its global empire, similar to the role played by the racist, anti-worker police and prison system inside the United States. The imperialist occupations of oppressed nations around the world mirror the reality for oppressed communities within the United States. In recent decades, under the pretext of the "war on drugs," whole communities of Black and Latino young people have been locked away, turning the U.S. government into the world's biggest jailer.

The past century has shown that imperialism is simultaneously at its most dangerous and most vulnerable when at war. For socialists in the advanced capitalist countries, opposition to imperialist war and support for the right of self-determination of countries targeted by one's "own" ruling class must be a top priority. This opposition is based on the irreconcilability of the interests of the working class, which must sacrifice and die in these wars, with the imperialists' interests—their drive for profit and domination.

CRISIS REVEALS REALITY: THE DICTATORSHIP OF THE RICH

Modern economic crises have exposed key aspects of the present system that formerly remained largely hidden from view in "ordinary" times.

For example, the capitalist crisis that began in 2007 and its aftermath demolished the myth of "free enterprise," proving instead that the U.S. system is the most corrupt form of capitalism that has ever existed. Without massive intervention by the federal government in the form of trillions of dollars in direct grants, loans and loan guarantees, the entire private finance/banking sector and many other major corporations would have collapsed.

The bank bailouts showed that while the government rules over the people, the banks rule over the government. Not only were the biggest banks each given tens of billions of dollars, they were not required to report on how they were going to use the money. The CEOs and other top bank executives awarded themselves huge bonuses out of the bailout funds despite their businesses failing.

The bailouts proved that the long-propagated notion that "the money is not there" for health care, education, housing and other social programs is a lie. Had the bailout money been used to meet people's needs, all of the unemployed people in the United States could have been hired at a living wage. Instead, the capitalist government continued to slash vital food, health, education, rehabilitation and other services.

The idea that any contemporary economic system can survive without major government intervention has been shown to be a total fallacy. The remaining question is not whether government intervention is necessary, but which class will benefit—the vast majority of society, the working class, or a tiny minority, the super rich?

Above all, the economic crisis has revealed that behind a façade of "democracy" the United States today is a dictatorship of the capitalist class. This reality will not change without a socialist revolution. The oppressors have never surrendered their power voluntarily.

THE U.S. WORKING CLASS TODAY

The technological revolution that has continued to this day has fundamentally changed the social composition of the U.S. working class, contributing to the possibilities of unity and the building of a revolutionary movement.

The overall effect of the high-tech revolution has been the deskilling of many job categories accompanied by ruthless wage-cutting. This has dramatically affected the living conditions of formerly privileged sectors of the white, male working class. It has also meant a more abundant army of the unemployed and underemployed, disproportionately hitting the Black and Latino communities.

A third of the workforce is non-white and half are women. This unintended effect of capitalism's drive for greater profits is creating its own gravediggers.

Since its formation, the U.S. bourgeoisie consciously created a complex system of white supremacy and apartheid to prevent class-wide unity and rebellion by all oppressed and exploited sectors of society. Over and above the genocide carried out against Native peoples, the enslavement of African peoples and its racist ideological justifications have been central to both extracting super-profits from the oppressed nationalities within the United States as well as preventing the multinational working class from acting in its own interests.

The collective experience of the civil rights, women's, immigrant rights and LGBT movements is now blended into the U.S. working-class experience and is something to draw from as it gains consciousness of itself. The critical role that racism, sexism and anti-

The basis for multinational working-class unity
is more apparent than ever before.

LGBT bigotry play in dividing workers continues to exist—but the material basis for overcoming these divisions is greater.

More importantly, it is now objectively possible to build a unified workers' movement with a multinational leadership. In fact, the very real opportunity of political leadership by the historically most oppressed sectors puts the working class today in a stronger position to struggle for power.

THE RIGHT OF REVOLUTION

The present form of government is destructive of the rights of the great majority. It is not a government "of, by and for the people." The existing government and state—the military, police, intelligence agencies, courts, prisons, bureaucracy and so on—defend the interests of the capitalist class. Racist, anti-working-class police brutality is rampant. A monstrous state machine has imprisoned more people in the United States than in any other country.

The existing state apparatus and government institutions were established to protect and defend the interests of the capitalist ruling class. The much-heralded system of "checks and balances" is really an undemocratic means of protecting the rich against the poor.

At every level of government, from the presidency to city councils, elections have become exercises in "dollar democracy." Corruption is business as usual—corporate lobbyists buy legislators' votes on a daily basis. All the important decisions are made behind closed doors, with the "debates" nothing more than a public show.

The federal court system comprised of appointed-for-life judges has vast powers to overturn legislation and is dedicated above all to safeguarding the rights of private property.

The capitalist system has proven to be incapable of meeting the needs of the people—even in the richest capitalist country in history. Every year, millions more people are forced into abject poverty, many while working full time, and many are denied the right to a job.

Simply reforming the capitalist system is not enough.

For the capitalists, reforms are a threat to the status quo. Reforms for the working class mean something different. They ease the burdens of living under capitalism through the extension of civil rights or other beneficial social or economic policies.

While reforms must be fought for, and can be won, they are under constant attack by the ruling class. Capitalism itself cannot be reformed. Its supreme law and driving force is the maximization of profit. The only force capable of putting an end to this criminal system is the organized working class. Capitalism cannot be voted out of power—it will take a revolution.

The capitalist class will stop at nothing to prevent or overturn reforms by repressing, misdirecting or quelling any form of popular rebellion. Without a complete uprooting of the system that causes all the problems workers and oppressed peoples face, exploitation and oppression will still exist. The capitalist state will continue to rule.

Capitalism is a failed system that, in its insatiable appetite for ever greater profits, threatens global ecological destruction on an unprecedented scale, with workers and oppressed people bearing the disproportionate burden of the environmental disaster.

More than at any other time, it is the working class that holds the future for humanity. For the people and planet to live, capitalism must go.

The Party for Socialism and Liberation is dedicated to building a revolutionary workers' party in the United States. A party that can unite the multinational U.S. working class is an essential and irreplaceable element in the struggle for socialism. The PSL participates in the labor, anti-war, anti-racist, immigrant rights, women's, lesbian/gay/bi/transgender, environmental, student and other movements. A revolutionary party can be built only by engaging in all issues affecting the working class.

For the working class, revolution is a necessity and a right. The most brutal aspects of capitalism will not go away unless there is a socialist revolution. Only a revolution can do away with the rule of the capitalists once and for all.

SOCIALISM AND COMMUNISM

The aim of the PSL is to abolish the corrupt, rotten and anti-people capitalist economy, state and governmental system, and replace it with one dedicated to meeting the needs of the people—a socialist system.

Solving the multiple crises of the present system is impossible without a revolution that ends the rule of the capitalist class and replaces it with a new state power that acts in the interest of the working class. Marx wrote, "The working class cannot simply lay hold of the ready-made state machinery and wield it for its own purposes." In other words, the government that has worked so well for the capitalists cannot serve the interests of the working class. The dictatorship of the rich must be dismantled and replaced with the working class in power. A state and government "of, by and for" the workers must replace the capitalist state.

The foundation of any state power is repressive force—the military, police, prisons, courts and so on. The standing army and police must be disbanded and replaced by the armed people, organized in workers' defense councils. A critical task of the new socialist order will be defending itself from the displaced capitalist class that would like to return to the days of exploitation.

A workers' government would create an entirely different type of court system, with its basic institutions determined by the democratic organs of workers' power. Judges would not be required to be lawyers.

All public officials, without exception, would be elected and subject to recall at any time by those who elected them. The salaries of all elected officials will be no higher than the average wage of workers. The same would be true for all those hired to carry out

*Corporate profits rule under capitalism;
socialism prioritizes meeting human needs.*

government and state business. Holding public office would be based on a real desire to serve, not on self-enrichment. Corporate lobbying would be eliminated—along with the corporations themselves.

A workers' government would begin to build socialism by expropriating the privatized wealth of the banks, industry, agribusiness, mines and other wealth-generating properties, eliminating the vast control the capitalists have over production. This would be done without compensation to the capitalist owners who have stolen so much for so long from the workers and oppressed peoples of the world.

Converting the private property of society to socially owned property is a necessary first step in building socialism by utilizing the productive capacity of society and natural resources of the planet for the benefit of humanity.

Whereas the goal of capitalist production is to make as much profit as quickly as possible, the goal of a planned socialist economy is to meet the needs of the people in a long-term and sustainable fashion. Workers would have access to more of what society produces. Planning is critical for socialist development.

Under capitalism, each corporation plans how much goods and services to produce and sell in order to maximize profits. But there is no overall plan to decide how to allocate society's finite resources, what should be produced, or what should be cut back or eliminated. The result is an enormous waste of resources, while the basic needs of billions go unmet.

Socialism is the necessary stage between capitalism and communism. The full achievement of socialism will require the development of the economy to meet the fundamental needs of the working class and the population as a whole. It will also be marked by the fading away of classes and class antagonisms. This cannot happen overnight.

Socialists use the term "private property" to refer to the system of capitalism—that is, the private ownership of the means of production: the factories, the land, the natural resources, such as oil and water, and the machinery to produce privately owned wealth. Under socialism, a home is regarded as personal property, not as a commodity for investment. Under socialism, housing would be a guaranteed right, and no individual would be able to own another person's home.

Ironically, under capitalism, the system that claims to uphold the sacred right of private property, homelessness has become a permanent feature and millions of people are losing their homes through foreclosures. But, for example, in socialist Cuba, despite being blockaded by the United States, there is no homelessness because a home is considered a human right. This was only possible through the elimination of "private property," including landlordism.

Achieving fully developed socialism, a goal that has not yet been achieved anywhere, will open the way to communism and the end of class society. Communism will also mean the "withering away" of the repressive state, which only came into being with the rise of class society.

Socialism can only be achieved by a mass movement of millions of people organized to fight for what is rightfully theirs. In working to build the movement that will usher in the next revolution—a socialist revolution—the PSL puts forward the following struggle-based program. This program outlines what a genuine workers' government would do. □

Part 2

A new government of working and poor people

IN order to guarantee the interests of working and poor people who make up the vast majority of the United States, a new revolutionary government run by and for the workers and poor shall be established. The present capitalist government—the role of which has been to defend the big-business system of exploitation by a web of hundreds of measures, legal and illegal, and has been accessible only to the super-rich elite—shall be abolished.

- The primary function of the new government shall be planning and administering the economy in the interests of working and poor people, as set forth below, and implementing the measures to fulfill those interests.
- Participation and representation in the new government shall be guaranteed through democratically organized workplace, neighborhood and social committees. The "professional politicians" and big-business political parties shall be replaced with the political organization of the working class.
- There shall be no distinction between the legislative and executive functions of government. Those who enact measures shall be responsible for carrying them out. All elected representatives shall be subject to recall at any time by the bodies that elect them.
- Elected officials of the new workers' government shall be paid an average worker's salary and shall receive no special privileges.
- There shall be primary government institutions created guaranteeing representation of all nationalities inside the United States. In recognition of centuries of national oppression and systematic exclusion, and to protect the interests of all, the new

government structures would be constructed to assure equal representation from all nationalities in the United States.

- The current legal and criminal justice system is infested with racism and class privilege, and shall be replaced by a new justice system based on the democratic organization of the working class and its right to defend its class interests on the basis of solidarity and unity.

- The rights of freedom of speech and political involvement shall be extended to the entire working class. These rights shall only be abridged in the efforts to eliminate racism, xenophobia and all forms of bigotry, or to prevent the re-establishment of the capitalist system of exploitation and oppression.

- There shall be a complete separation of church and state, with no one religion favored over another and no favoring of religion over the absence of religion.

- No law shall be enacted that discriminates against people based on nationality, gender, sexual orientation or gender expression. The new government shall take it as the highest priority to remedy the legacy of institutionalized divisions and inequalities perpetuated against wide sectors of the working class that had continued without respite for hundreds of years, by measures of affirmative action and other measures listed below.

- Older and retired workers will be able to live a dignified and fulfilling life with the constitutionally guaranteed rights to housing, health care, food and water. The new government will allocate resources to ensure the maximum participation in society of older and retired workers. The new government shall initiate an educational campaign to promote respect for older people and to value their contributions to society.

- People with disabilities will be guaranteed full access to, and participation in, society, with the government allocating resources to eliminate barriers in housing, education, employment and public facilities. The new government shall initiate an educational campaign to promote respect for and programs in the interests of people with disabilities, promoting their contributions to society.

- The new government will place great importance on the social development of children. The new government will allocate

Measures like affirmative action will help
overcome the legacy of racism and discrimination.

resources to develop programs for the intellectual, physical, psychological and social development of young people.

- The defense of the revolutionary government shall be organized on the basis of the armed, organized working class. All foreign military bases shall be closed immediately.
- The new government will approach the peoples of the world on the principles of international working-class solidarity. All occupations, military interventions and military proxy wars, agreements and alliances carried out by the previous imperialist government shall be ended immediately.

- A national assembly shall craft a new Constitution that enshrines and protects the interests of workers and oppressed peoples, to address, at minimum, the issues outlined below.

SOCIALISM: ADDRESSING THE INTERESTS OF WORKING AND POOR PEOPLE

The new government shall be directed to address the interests of working and poor people. This means that no laws, regulations or measures shall negatively impact the rights of working and poor people in society. The following issues will be addressed by the new government.

- The exploitation of labor for private profit shall be prohibited.
- It shall be a right of every person in the United States to have a job with guaranteed union representation and full social benefits provided by the new government, including a pension, health care, workers' compensation, paid parental and family leave for up to one year, a minimum of one month's paid vacation, and at least 12 paid holidays and sick days.
- Poverty shall be eradicated by providing a guaranteed living income for any worker who is not able to find or hold a job. Priority in addressing the legacy of capitalism shall be granted to communities that have suffered disproportionately in the past.
- Citizenship rights shall be granted to every person living in the United States. No person shall be discriminated against in any way due to past citizenship status.
- Working conditions shall aim to enhance the humanity and dignity of all workers. The working week shall be 30 hours. Child care for workers shall be provided by the new government at no cost to the parents. There shall be cultural and athletic opportunities for all workers during working hours.
- The new government shall provide free, high-quality health care to every person living in the United States, regardless of citizenship. For-profit health care and private insurance companies shall be outlawed.
- The new government shall provide decent housing for every person in the United States. No person shall pay more than 10 percent of their income on housing costs. It shall be illegal to

generate private profit by renting or selling land. No person may suffer foreclosure or eviction.

- The new government shall provide free, high-quality education to every person in the United States from pre-school through college, as well as post-college educational opportunities for life-long learning to advance the technical and cultural level of society, as well as the promotion of working-class unity and international solidarity. The historic disparities in educational quality and opportunities in Black, Latino, Asian and Native communities, and other working-class communities, shall be addressed as a first order of business. The intellectual products of colleges and universities shall be the property of society, with no patents, trademarks, copyrights or private profit from social knowledge and materials.

- The new government will approach agriculture by implementing sustainable methods. This means environmental protection; water and soil conservation; and improvement of the quality of

Homelessness will disappear under socialism as housing will be a right provided to all.

PHOTO: BILL HACKWELL

Cuba's planned economy has led to a superior record of sustainable development. Here, a community garden

life of agricultural laborers and rural communities by providing adequate wages, safe working conditions, year-round employment opportunities, housing, health care, education, social and recreational services, the elimination of "guest worker" programs and all laws discriminating against workers on the basis of citizenship, and humane treatment of animals.

- The food and nutritional needs of the population shall be the responsibility of the new government. All schools and workplaces shall provide high-quality meals to those who study or work there. It shall be illegal to profit from the production or distribution of food and food products. Food shall be produced according to a democratic and rational plan, with opportunities for the input of all people into what foods are produced and the manner in which they are produced and distributed.

- The new government shall recognize that the well-being of the environment is essential for the future development of the economy and society, indeed for all workers and oppressed people. Environmental considerations shall be made in every area of economic and social planning, and there shall be special efforts to remedy and end environmental degradation.

- Penal institutions shall be organized on the principle of social education and rehabilitation. Those convicted of unlawful acts shall maintain political rights while participating in their rehabilitation.

LIBERATION: OVERCOMING RACISM, EXPLOITATION, NATIONAL OPPRESSION AND ALL FORMS OF BIGOTRY

The new government shall seek to codify the goals of eradicating racism, national oppression and all forms of exploitation and bigotry. The following issues will be addressed by the new government.

- The new government shall recognize the inviolable right of all oppressed nations to self-determination with regard to their means of gaining and maintaining their liberation. In the United States, this includes the right of self-determination for African American, Native, Puerto Rican and other Latino national minorities, the Hawai'ian nation, Asian, Pacific Islander, Arab and other oppressed peoples who have experienced oppression as a whole people under capitalism.
- With the goal of the unity of the multinational U.S. working class on the basis of class solidarity, the new government shall eliminate white supremacy, racism and privilege as an immediate task, recognizing that this goal will not be achieved automatically or by decree. It shall be prohibited to advocate any form of racism, xenophobia or national hatred.
- The new government shall institute a program of reparations for the African American community to address the centuries of unpaid slave labor and super-exploitation.
- All U.S. colonies shall be granted independence, including Puerto Rico, Samoa, Guam, the Virgin Islands and the Mariana Islands. The new government shall honor all treaty obligations with Native nations, and shall provide restitution for land and resources stolen by the capitalist U.S. government.
- The new government shall institute programs on the basis of proletarian internationalism to help overcome the ravages of U.S. imperialism that have exploited the people, resources and

economies of other countries with an emphasis on sovereignty, solidarity, revolutionary assistance and reparations.

• All U.S. workers shall have the right to speak the language of their choosing. All government services and education shall be provided with multilingual provisions.

• Sexism and other forms of male chauvinism and oppression of women shall be eliminated as an immediate task, recognizing that this goal will not be achieved automatically or by decree. It shall be prohibited to advocate any form of sexism or male chauvinism.

• The new government shall guarantee the right of women workers to receive the same pay, benefits and treatment as their male counterparts.

• The right to contraception, birth control and abortion services shall not be restricted in any way, nor shall there be any restriction on a woman's right to decide to have children or not. Abortion services shall be available free and on demand.

• It shall be the responsibility of the new government to provide women with the right to choose to have children by providing free, high-quality pre- and post-natal health care and child care. Any caregiver shall be given access to free child care.

• All forms of bigotry, discrimination or the promotion of hatred against lesbians, gays, bisexuals and transgender people, or against anyone on the basis of their sexual orientation or gender expression, shall be eliminated, including in marriage rights, employment, housing, adoption and health care. It shall be prohibited to advocate any form of bigotry, discrimination or hatred against LGBT people.

• No law or measure shall give preference in word or in deed that favors heterosexual relationships over other relationships.

• There shall be a sustained public education campaign promoting the goals of multinational working-class unity and international solidarity, the advancement of women's rights, the promotion of respect of sexual orientation and gender expression, as well as exposing the evils of racism, sexism, anti-LGBT bigotry, xenophobia and national chauvinism. Affirmative action measures shall be instituted wherever needed to eliminate the effects of historical discrimination in education, employment, promotion, housing and other areas.

CONCLUSION

There are only two choices for humanity today: an increasingly destructive capitalism, or socialism. The PSL believes that the only solution to the evils of capitalism is the socialist transformation of society. The program outlined above is just the beginning of what can be achieved when workers and oppressed people organize and take power.

The people of the United States desperately need and deserve a new government and a new system run by the multinational working class in their interests. The struggle to defeat capitalism and begin building a socialist society is the most pressing issue faced by humanity today. □

Who We Are, What We Stand For

Introduction

THE Party for Socialism and Liberation believes that the only solution to the deepening crisis of capitalism is the socialist transformation of society. Driven by an insatiable appetite for ever greater profits regardless of social cost, capitalism is on a collision course with the people of the world and the planet itself. Imperialist war; deepening unemployment and poverty; deteriorating health care, housing and education; racism; discrimination and violence based on gender and sexual orientation; environmental destruction—all are inevitable products of the capitalist system itself.

For the great majority of people in the world, including tens of millions of workers in the United States, conditions of life and work are worsening. There is no prospect that this situation can or will be turned around under the existing system.

The idea that the capitalists' grip on society and their increasingly repressive state can be abolished through any means other than a revolutionary overturn is an illusion. Equally unrealistic are reformist hopes for a "kinder, gentler" capitalism, or solutions based on economic decentralization or small group autonomy. Meeting the needs of the more than 6.5 billion people who inhabit the planet today is impossible without large-scale agriculture and industry and economic planning.

The fundamental problems confronting humanity today flow from the reality that most of the world's productive wealth—the product of socialized labor and nature—is privately owned and controlled by a tiny minority. This minority decides what will be produced and what will not. Its decisions are based on making profits rather than meeting human needs.

There are really only two choices for humanity today—an increasingly destructive capitalism, or socialism.

The need for socialism, a system based on meeting people's needs through common ownership of the productive wealth and a planned, sustainable economy, becomes more urgent every day. Socialism can only be achieved by the conscious, organized and united action of the working class. To win, the working class needs its own party.

The Party for Socialism and Liberation was formed in the summer of 2004 by leading organizers and activists experienced in a wide range of struggles. Since its formation, the PSL has experienced significant growth in cadres, regional presence and organizational development. We are moving forward with the task of building a revolutionary Marxist party based on the working class, and we seek unity with all those who agree with our perspective. Such a party must not only look to a different future. It must be engaged in all of today's struggles against oppression and exploitation.

The PSL is committed to the struggle for socialism. Under the current system, the big capitalist owners—a miniscule fraction of the population—dominate society. We fight for a society in which the working class, the vast majority, holds power. Only when the tremendous wealth of society is owned by the many who created it, rather than the few who now hold legal title to it, will it be possible to speak about democracy in any realistic way.

In place of an economic system based on maximizing profits, we stand for an economy based on meeting people's needs in a way that is environmentally sustainable. The resources exist to guarantee every person on Earth the right to employment, adequate food, clean water, health care, housing, education, cultural activities and more. But these basic needs will never be met as long as control of the productive wealth and resources remains in the hands of the capitalists.

Capitalism thrives on oppression and division along the lines of nationality, gender, sexual orientation, immigration status, age, ability/disability and religion. We seek a new society based on equality and solidarity among all people.

Instead of endless war, capitalist globalization and imperialist domination, the PSL stands for international cooperation, friendship and respect for the rights of all peoples and nations, large and small.

None of these aims can be achieved without abolishing the capitalist system and replacing it with socialism. □

Part 1

The validity of Marxism and Leninism

CONTRARY to the assertions of bourgeois academics and right-wing pundits who have long proclaimed Marxism "dead," contemporary reality every day reaffirms the validity of Karl Marx's fundamental analysis and prognosis.

In "Capital," Volume 1, written in 1867, Marx described the process of capitalist development: "Accumulation of wealth at one pole is, therefore, at the same time accumulation of misery ... at the opposite pole." As the rich get richer, the poor get poorer.

In the Communist Manifesto, Marx and Engels wrote:

"The need of a constantly expanding market for its products chases the bourgeoisie over the whole surface of the globe. It must nestle everywhere, settle everywhere, establish connections everywhere. ... The bourgeoisie, through its exploitation of the world market, gives a cosmopolitan character to production and consumption in every country. ... It compels all nations, on pain of extinction, to adopt a bourgeois mode of production. It compels them to introduce what it calls civilization into their midst, in other words to become bourgeois themselves. ... In a word, it creates a world after its own image."

These words, which so eloquently describe the process known today as "globalization," were written in 1848, before there were telephones, cars or planes, not to mention microchips, computers and wireless communications.

Lenin's analysis of imperialism as the final stage of capitalism retains all of its force and relevance, as does his prediction shortly after the start of World War I:

"Humanity must either pass over to Socialism, or for years, nay, decades, witness armed conflicts of the 'great' nations for artificial maintenance of capitalism by means of colonies, monopolies, privileges and all sorts of national oppression." The contemporary U.S. occupations of, wars or threats of war against Iraq, Afghanistan, Palestine, Cuba, former Yugoslavia, Colombia, Korea, Venezuela, Iran, Sudan, Philippines and other countries affirm Lenin's prognosis.

Imperialist aggression and capitalist exploitation continue regardless of whether it is the Democrats or Republicans who control the White House and Congress. The capitalist state, as Marx and Lenin analyzed it, remains an instrument of class oppression that is impossible to reform, an instrument of corporate rule. To create a new and just society, a socialist society, it is necessary to dismantle the repressive capitalist state and replace it with one that serves the interests of working people.

The major contradictions of capitalism that Marx and Lenin illuminated—the struggle between the classes, the struggle between oppressor and oppressed nations and so on—have intensified in recent years due to the counterrevolutions in Eastern Europe and the Soviet Union, what Fidel Castro called the greatest setback in the history of the working class. □

Part 2

The U.S. drive for global domination

OUR starting point in assessing the state of the class struggle in the United States is the world situation. The U.S. ruling class, its government and its military establishment together constitute the most powerful and destructive force in the world today. It is the main obstacle to real progress in the "developing world." Since emerging from World War II as the leading world power, the fixed aim of U.S. international policy has been unrivaled global domination.

From 1945 to 1989, Washington pursued this aim by means of covert operations, coups, nuclear blackmail and numerous invasions and interventions on nearly every continent. The greatest obstacle standing in the way of achieving their goal was the existence of the socialist camp, centered in the Soviet Union.

The destruction of the socialist camp between 1989 and 1991 brought disastrous changes for the peoples of Eastern Europe and the USSR, and profound challenges for the socialist governments of North Korea, Cuba, Vietnam, Laos and (then) Yugoslavia. It radically changed the worldwide relationship of forces. In the new unipolar world, U.S. imperialism was able to exert economic as well as military pressure, particularly in the form of sanctions, far more effectively against Iraq, Yugoslavia, Vietnam, Libya, Iran, Cuba and others.

The counterrevolution in Europe and the Soviet Union also accelerated a sharp turn to the right in China, following the defeat of the 1989 counterrevolutionary attempt in Beijing.

THE OVERTHROW OF THE SOVIET UNION

The 1991 overthrow and dissolution of the Soviet Union as a political and social entity by leaders and former leaders of the Communist Party of the Soviet Union was an unparalleled catastrophe for the working class inside and outside the USSR. Heralded by world imperialism as the final triumph of capitalism over socialism, this counterrevolutionary overthrow strengthened the hand of U.S. imperialism in its march for economic, political and military domination of the entire planet.

The socialist experiment that began in 1917 took place under the most difficult circumstances. Socialist economic development needs peace more than all else. Yet the USSR faced unrelenting war and the threat of war from its birth. Fourteen imperialist countries, including the United States, Britain, Germany and Japan, invaded Soviet territory after the revolutionary triumph. They used every means including total economic blockade to "strangle the Bolshevik baby in its crib," in the words of British imperialist leader Winston Churchill.

Lenin and the other Bolshevik leaders never anticipated that the Russian Revolution would be forced to go it alone. They viewed their revolution as the first crest of a revolutionary wave that, they hoped, would engulf Europe and eventually the world. Revolutions in the more advanced capitalist countries, particularly Germany, would provide essential assistance to Russia, and open the way for a new socialist federation. But while there were revolutionary upheavals in Germany, Hungary, Bulgaria and other countries between 1918 and 1923, none succeeded in securing working-class power for more than a short period. The missing ingredient in each case was an experienced revolutionary party of the Bolshevik type.

The Soviet state was left on its own to confront seemingly insurmountable tasks at home and internationally. That it survived at all in the face of imperialist encirclement and the massive destruction of its productive forces in World War I and the civil war that followed the revolution, and with a population that was overwhelmingly in the countryside, was near miraculous.

Socialist construction began in Russia in the 1920s. But the achievement of socialism in the full sense, the original Bolshevik leaders believed, would only be possible when capitalism was overthrown on a world scale. The transition from socialism to the higher stage of communism requires the withering away of the state. As long as inherently aggressive capitalism and imperialism continue to exist in most of the world, the workers' states must remain strong.

The Soviet Red Army dealt a decisive blow to the Nazi war machine at Stalingrad, February 1943.

After less than two decades of relative peace, the Soviet Union was once again attacked in 1941, this time by the most powerful military machine ever assembled up to that time. At an almost unimaginable cost—27 million people killed and two-thirds of its productive capacity destroyed—the USSR smashed the Nazi menace.

Following World War II, the Soviet Union was immediately plunged into a severe and costly nuclear and conventional arms race. On top of this, the USSR faced endless economic sabotage, sanctions and CIA operations in every sphere.

Given the pressures applied to this first socialist state, its accomplishments will be remembered in history as extraordinary. Its example and lessons, both positive and negative, will be a starting point for the revival of the world communist movement.

The Soviet Union was not simply a "second superpower" capable of competing and checking imperialist global domination. The Soviet Union rested on an entirely different social structure following the expropriation of the capitalists and the big landowner class after the triumph of the 1917 Russian Revolution.

The means of production were public property. The economy was operated according to central planning rather than being driven by the law of maximizing profit. The economy was protected from the ravages of imperialist economic penetration by the erection of a comprehensive monopoly of foreign trade. These distinguishing features separated the Soviet social system from all the capitalist powers. They also allowed the Soviet Union to develop on an entirely different class basis and provided the social foundation for stupendous economic gains, in spite of repeated invasions, endless economic sanctions and nuclear military threats, feats unmatched by any other "poor country" in the 20th century.

Although the legacy of principled revolutionary internationalism eroded in the decades following the death of Lenin in 1924, the Soviet Union under various leaderships gave military and economic assistance to countries fighting for national liberation from colonialism and semi-colonialism. Its aid and support for Cuba, Vietnam and North Korea was an essential component in their struggles for

Soviet aid and favorable trade relations helped the Cuban Revolution advance. Here, a Cuban factory built with Soviet assistance

PHOTO: PEDRO BERUVIDES/GRANMA

national liberation. The mere existence of the Soviet bloc provided an alternative source for economic trade and military alliances that were indispensable. In Africa, the USSR gave economic and military assistance to the revolutionary movements in South Africa, Angola, Mozambique and elsewhere.

The Soviet leadership in the USSR had a two-fold and contradictory character. After the Russian Revolution, a ruling stratum or bureaucracy developed, which directed the management of the economic, military and political apparatus of the state machine. To the extent that the bureaucracy developed the country's material foundations and defended those foundations from domestic counter-revolution and imperialist intervention, it assumed a necessary and progressive function. But as a stratum or caste that accumulated privilege and justified inequality both on a political and ideological basis, the Soviet bureaucracy also became a principal instrument for capitalist restorationist tendencies within society. These trends were strengthened in the ideological sphere by the official promotion and replacement of the theory of class struggle with a bourgeois notion: the "theory of peaceful co-existence."

Following World War II, each successive generation of party cadres was educated in this overarching theory. Its core message was that the main problem in the modern world was not the class struggle against capitalism and imperialism and the need for its replacement by socialism but rather the need to establish long-term peace between the socialist and the imperialist countries. Successive Soviet generations were schooled in the anti-Marxist conception that another world war could be avoided and world peace secured by politically checking the far right-wing militarists inside world imperialism and promoting the ascension of the moderate or peaceful imperialists.

Advocates of "peaceful co-existence" pointed to the unparalleled losses suffered by the USSR in World War II, and the fact that the U.S. pursued a "first-strike" nuclear war strategy against the USSR. But no theory could alter the inherently aggressive character of imperialism.

The conception of "peaceful co-existence" as a long-term strategic objective, promoted as the official doctrine of the Communist Party of the Soviet Union for many years, reached its apex in the late 1980s. Mikhail Gorbachev, the CPSU's general secretary, abandoned the theory of the proletarian class struggle altogether. He announced that capitalism and socialism could merge into a single system based on the mutual embrace of overarching human values. Under the mantle of perestroika (economic restructuring) and glasnost (openness), Gorbachev introduced far-reaching capitalist market reforms in the economic sphere while carrying out a vast purge of pro-communist elements in the Soviet bureaucracy, replacing them with openly pro-capitalist figures such as Boris Yeltsin. The most rabidly right-wing forces, with the open support of U.S. imperialism and every other capitalist power, waged a final decapitating struggle against the pro-communist forces inside the leadership, leading to the dissolution of the USSR.

While the capitalist restorationist wing of the CPSU struggled for power between 1988 and 1991, the great Soviet working class remained atomized, largely leaderless and passive in the face of this monumental assault on their social system. For decades, all tendencies within the Soviet bureaucracy had muffled any open political struggle, weakening the political power of the working class. Consequently, pro-socialist elements within the bureaucracy were incapable of mobilizing the working class in a decisive struggle against the counterrevolution. Instead, confusion reigned.

Although the working class and collective farmers had voted overwhelmingly to maintain the Soviet Union in a March 1991 national referendum, the working class remained largely passive as the two factions of the CPSU fought it out in the summer of 1991. With the backing of U.S. imperialism and its NATO allies, Boris Yeltsin took power and dissolved the USSR.

Not only have the working people of the former Soviet Union lost many of their social and economic rights since 1991, the country itself has been reduced on all levels. Many of the former Soviet republics now house U.S. and NATO military bases, and the country's natural and industrial resources have been looted by capitalist vultures. For those oppressed countries in the world that relied on the Soviet bloc as an alternative trading partner in the world economy, their status has been reduced to extreme economic colonialism, as the International Monetary Fund moved in to rapidly enforce Structural Adjustment Programs as a condition for the extension of credit in the world capitalist economy.

While the apologists for the current social order use the overthrow of the Soviet Union as supposed proof that socialism and communism are either impossible or simply a utopian fantasy, the opposite will prove to be the case. The dissolution of socialist property relations has caused immense poverty, homelessness, unemployment, crime, drug use, prostitution, and the rise of venomous internal ethnic and national strife—all the commonplace features of capitalism that were largely absent prior to 1991.

To their lasting discredit, some so-called "socialist" organizations in the United States and elsewhere joined in the world bourgeoisie's celebration of the demise of the Soviet Union, labeling it as a "victory for democracy" or the "defeat of Stalinism."

THE IMPACT ON SOCIALIST CONSTRUCTION

The elimination of the Soviet Union from the world scene has had a profound impact on all the countries that have undertaken the historic task of building socialism. This has been true both for the countries that relied on the USSR for material aid as well as those that tried to build socialism outside of the Soviet framework.

The Democratic People's Republic of Korea, the Socialist Republic of Vietnam and the People's Democratic Republic of Laos embarked on building socialism under the most difficult conditions. All faced massive human and economic devastation in defending their revolutions against U.S. imperialist military intervention. All benefited substantially from the Soviet Union's military and economic aid in order to rebuild and defend themselves. All—particularly North Korea—find themselves on the defensive since the downfall of the USSR.

The People's Republic of China did not have the same dependence on Soviet aid, a result of the debilitating Sino-Soviet split of the 1960s. Today, at the same time that China is led by the Communist Party of China and very significant state-controlled sectors of the economy remain, capitalism has made political and economic inroads. The CPC's contradictory policy of "market socialism" has opened the country to international capital and the growth of a Chinese bourgeoisie. Its long-term high level of annual economic growth has made China the world's second-largest economy.

As China plays a growing role in the world economy, inequality within China is also on the rise. The CPC has long abandoned a revolutionary internationalist foreign policy. But U.S. imperialism increasingly views China not just as a market and source of labor, but also as a strategic competitor. The prospect of an eventual U.S. war with China is openly discussed by sectors of the U.S. ruling class, which views China as a potential future challenger of U.S. global domination. The U.S. government continues its intervention in China's internal affairs, arming the regime in Taiwan and supporting secessionist movements in Tibet and western China.

Taiwan is part of an arc of U.S. military bases and, air and sea forces encircling China. Imperialism would support a counterrevolution in China, just as it did in 1989 when the U.S. ruling class sought to turn a protracted, multi-issue demonstration in Beijing's Tiananmen Square into a counterrevolutionary civil war.

REVOLUTIONARY CUBA

For more than five decades, spanning 11 U.S. presidencies, the U.S. ruling class has waged war on revolutionary Cuba. Military invasion, espionage, terrorism, biological warfare, economic blockade, diplomatic attacks and more have been utilized in the unrelenting campaign to recapture the only truly independent territory in the Americas.

Throughout the most severe difficulties and suffering brought on by the fall of the socialist camp, the Communist Party of Cuba has affirmed its unbreakable allegiance to revolution, Marxism, and the cause of the workers and oppressed peoples of the world. In the most difficult days of the "Special Period in Time of Peace" in the mid-1990s, when everything was in direly short supply, then-Cuban President Fidel Castro proclaimed "Socialism or death."

Even when beset by the gravest shortages, Cuba, a country of 11.5 million people, never halted its internationalist projects. The most renowned was sending 300,000 volunteers to Angola in the 1970s and 1980s to fight the South African army. These volunteers played a key role in defeating the South African forces, including at the decisive battle of Cuito Cuanavale. That victory led directly to the liberation of Namibia and contributed to the dismantling of legal apartheid in South Africa.

After 1995, the Cuban economy stabilized and made modest but very real steps forward. While forced to allow foreign investment

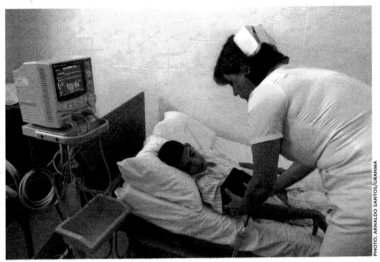

Cuba's socialist health care system provides
free health care for all citizens.

and some small-scale private ownership to compensate for the grave losses in trade and assistance suffered due to the dissolution of the socialist camp, the Cuban government has carried out these reforms in a careful and controlled fashion, and has cancelled a number of them when they were deemed harmful to the socialist system. The state has reasserted itself to strengthen the socialist foundations to the extent that the economy has improved. Deprived of its former socialist trading partners, Cuba's economy is heavily impacted by the ups and downs of global capitalism.

Having failed to crush Cuba by tightening the blockade during its most difficult times, the U.S. government has embarked upon a new series of measures designed to cause greater hardships, step up internal counterrevolutionary activity and heighten tensions between the two countries, possibly leading to military confrontation.

U.S. IMPERIALISM'S STRATEGIC OBJECTIVE: GLOBAL DOMINATION

The destruction of the USSR and the socialist governments in Eastern Europe heightened the Pentagon's aggressiveness and led to a stepped-up U.S. drive for unrivaled global supremacy.

A new series of wars and interventions followed in quick succession: Panama, Iraq, Somalia, Haiti, Sudan, Afghanistan, Yugoslavia and Iraq again.

New threats were made against North Korea, Iran, Syria, Venezuela, Cuba and other countries that were seen as not in compliance with the "new order." U.S. "advisors" were sent into Colombia, the Philippines and other countries to conduct counter-insurgency operations against popular resistance movements.

The Pentagon today has 750 bases in more than 100 countries worldwide.

The destruction of the Soviet Union not only meant impoverishment and bloody strife for the peoples of that multinational state. It also eliminated the main brake on unlimited U.S. military aggression around the world. The dramatic shift in the global relationship of forces led to the implementation of a doctrine of global domination first outlined in a 1992 Pentagon document.

The pillars of this doctrine, which has taken on various names over time, are: 1) U.S. financial/commercial domination through the International Monetary Fund, World Bank, World Trade Organization, North American Free Trade Agreement and so on; 2) absolute military superiority achieved through a war budget that exceeds the military expenditures of all other countries in the world combined; and 3) control of global resources, particularly oil, and strategic positions.

Under this strategic conception there must be one and only one "superpower"—the United States. U.S. global supremacy must be unchallenged and unchallengeable. It targets oppressed and former colonized countries, especially in key strategic regions.

At the same time, U.S. strategy has also been aimed at curtailing the markets and power of its imperialist rivals/allies, such as Germany, France, Italy, Japan, Britain and others. Imperialist rivalry manifests itself in many areas and forms. The conflicts in Central Africa, battles over trade quotas and government subsidies of agriculture and industry, the dispute over the Iraq war—all are manifestations of the rivalry between the imperialist powers for access to world markets and resources. In the aftermath of World War II, the British ruling class was forced to accept both the reality that its power had declined as well as a new role as U.S. junior partner. After its defeat by the United States in 1945, the Japanese ruling class was forced to accommodate itself to a similar role.

The European Union, Japan and China all have growing energy deficits—shortages of oil—for which imports must compensate. Tightening U.S. military control over key sources of global oil resources as a consequence of the Afghanistan and Iraq wars is a key factor in U.S. strategic planning.

The attacks of Sept. 11, 2001, in New York and Washington, resulted in the killing of nearly 2,800 civilians. U.S. political leaders used the attacks as the pretext for the invasions of Afghanistan and Iraq, and the stepped-up U.S.-Israeli war against the Palestinian people.

Many times the number of civilians killed on Sept. 11 have since died in those wars, and the social infrastructure supporting life for millions of people has been destroyed. The U.S. military terrorizes entire peoples with high-tech weapons of mass destruction, and at the same time has increased the repression of the people in its own territory, in other imperialist countries and in dominated countries.

Yet time after time, imperialist war has also been the setting where revolutionary change is most possible. World War I cracked Russian imperial power and gave birth to the Bolshevik Revolution. In the wake of World War II, China, Yugoslavia, Vietnam and North Korea broke away from imperialist and capitalist domination, as did Bulgaria, Albania, Czechoslovakia, Romania, Hungary, Poland and East Germany.

THE STRUGGLE IN THE MIDDLE EAST

For the U.S ruling class, Iraq and the entire Persian/Arabian Gulf region is a prize it has sought since World War II. The conquest of Iraq was not only motivated by its rich oil resources, but was also seen as a key element in the virtual re-colonization of the entire region, which in turn was viewed as critical to the success of the strategy of U.S. global domination. There is no part of the world that the U.S. ruling class considers more critical than the Middle East.

The Washington perpetrators of the Iraq invasion and occupation promised that it would be a brief and easy operation. They argued, moreover, that it would lead to a fundamental reorganization of the region along lines favorable to imperialist interests. The Iraq

PHOTO: REUTERS/KHALEED AL-MOUSLY

U.S. troops still occupy Iraq.

war was to have a "demonstration effect;" it would "demonstrate" the futility of any other government even thinking about standing up to U.S. dictates. Instead, the rapid expansion of the Iraqi resistance— predictable but completely unanticipated by the arrogant Washington warlords—created a major crisis for the U.S. rulers. The occupation forces have inflicted immense casualties and destruction on both Iraq and Afghanistan, but have not succeeded in pacifying either country. For the empire, anything short of outright victory is a defeat.

U.S. attempts to bring about "regime change" in Lebanon, Syria and Iran have also so far failed, but these interventions are far from done.

Washington is particularly targeting Iran, using the pretext of "concern" over Iran's purported development of nuclear weapons, an objective the Iranian government denies. The fact that Iran is sur- rounded by nuclear weapons—from Pakistan, to India, Russia, Israel and the U.S. Navy—has not deterred the United States from proclaim- ing that "if Iran acquires nuclear weapons the whole region would be destabilized." This exercise in propaganda is designed to hide the real motives for the ratcheting up of the anti-Iran campaign: regime change and the neutralization of the last large state in the Gulf region not under U.S. domination.

The heroic struggle of the Palestinian people is inextricably tied to the battle in Iraq. In pursuit of its aim of total domination of the entire Middle East, the U.S. leaders have given the Israeli government a green light to crush the Palestinian struggle by whatever means it chooses. The extreme aggressiveness of Israeli policies, the annexations of large sections of the West Bank and the numerical equalizing

Palestinians throw stones at an Israeli army bulldozer in the West Bank city of Jenin.

PHOTO: AFP/SAIF DAHLAH

of Jewish and Palestinian populations in historic Palestine are factors that together have all but eliminated the possibility of a "two-state solution." The Israeli aim now is a new "transfer," or expulsion, of a large part of the Palestinian population, which will otherwise soon surpass the Israeli Jewish population.

The vast and multi-faceted support for Israel from the U.S. establishment has nothing to do with sympathy for Jewish people. Because of its settler-state character and dependence on assistance from the U.S. and Europe, Washington views Israel as a far more reliable defender of imperialist interests in the Middle East than any other state in the region. Even Arab countries with the most compliant regimes, it is feared in U.S. ruling circles, could be radically transformed by revolutionary developments. The overthrow of the Shah of Iran in 1979 and the United States' subsequent loss of Iran as a guardian of U.S. interests in the Persian/Arabian Gulf region, is still fresh in the minds of U.S. policy makers.

The problem of an overstretched U.S. army due to the wars in Iraq and Afghanistan highlights the continuing importance of Israel as a military garrison state serving the U.S. Empire in the Middle East. What would be the U.S.'s options in the event of a mass upheaval or governmental overthrow in a dependent Middle East state? Such a development is certainly not unthinkable given the unprecedented level of popular anger toward the United States and its client regimes in the Arab world. The brutal assaults on Lebanon in 2006 and Gaza in 2008 to 2009 should be understood as U.S.-Israeli offensives. While inflicting massive civilian casualties and damage, neither attack succeeded in achieving its real objective—destroying or dislodging the targeted movements.

LATIN AMERICA:
THE ALBA ALLIANCE RESISTS YANKEE DOMINATION

The tying down of significant U.S. military and other resources in the Iraq and Afghanistan wars has impacts far beyond the Middle East. In Latin America, the Bolivarian Alliance for Latin America (ALBA), an alliance of socialist and progressive nationalist governments, has grown stronger. ALBA began as an alliance between socialist Cuba and the progressive government led by Hugo Chávez in Venezuela, which has proclaimed its socialist aim as well. ALBA began as a response to the U.S.-led "Free Trade Area of the Americas." In reality, the FTAA is a plan for the complete subjugation of Latin America to U.S. interests.

Starting with two countries, ALBA has now expanded to include Bolivia, Ecuador, Nicaragua, Antigua and Barbuda, and St. Vincent and the Grenadines, with five other observer countries. Honduras joined ALBA in 2009, but just weeks later its government was overthrown in a military coup secretly backed by the United States.

It is clear that U.S. policy is aimed at regaining lost ground by undermining ALBA—especially targeting the two founding states, Cuba and Venezuela—by whatever means it deems necessary, including sanction, blockades, subversion, and covert and overt military action. To that end, Washington is going forward with a massive military build-up in Colombia, the main base of Pentagon/CIA operations in South America.

The PSL defends the right of self-determination and sovereignty not only for socialist states but also for all oppressed states and nations that are the victims of imperialist attack. The fight against national chauvinism is essential to advancing class consciousness in the U.S. working class. Failure to fulfill this elementary duty disqualifies any party from being regarded as progressive, much less revolutionary. □

Part 3

The U.S. working class today

THE PSL recognizes that the multinational U.S. working class is the indispensable force for revolution in the United States. Its social force is magnified by the central role of U.S. imperialism in the world economy. The task of breaking the chains of wage labor in the United States is intimately tied to the struggle of people around the world for national liberation and social revolution.

More and more, speaking in the United States of "foreign" versus "domestic" policy creates a false dichotomy. The occupations of Iraq and Afghanistan, for example, are not just "international" issues. They affect hundreds of thousands of working-class families across the United States—just as the Vietnam War did at an earlier time. Taken together, Washington's policies at home and abroad are integrated in a global war waged by U.S. imperialism against the workers and poor of the world.

"Endless war" against Yugoslavia, Iraq, Afghanistan, Palestine, Haiti and other countries inevitably means war against the multinational working class here as well. It is the sons and daughters of the working class, disproportionately people of color, who are subjected to an economic draft—fighting, killing and dying for the interests of profit and empire. Education, health care, public and subsidized housing, jobs and job training, welfare, child care and other vital social programs have been gutted, privatized or entirely eliminated as real military spending has risen above a half-trillion dollars annually. Social Security is on the chopping block.

Every new military adventure means an acceleration of the militarization of U.S. society and of other reactionary, anti-working-class trends.

U.S. militarism and imperialist globalization policies have a profound impact on the composition and conditions of the U.S. working class. With the gutting of national economies from Mexico to Haiti, for example, millions of workers have immigrated to the United States. In 2000, one in three residents of New York City was born outside the United States.

THE WORKING CLASS UNDER ATTACK

Living and working conditions have been declining for large sections of the U.S. working class for the past three decades in the face of a massive corporate offensive. The deterioration of real wages and benefits like health care and pensions is accelerating at a rate only matched by the increasing wealth hoarded by an ever smaller handful of banks and the super rich. There is no indication that this offensive is slowing. The U.S. and global capitalist economy is experiencing an unprecedented downturn. Tens of millions of workers are facing a deepening crisis of how to pay for the basic necessities of life—housing, food, clothing, medical care, child care and education.

The high-tech revolution that began in the 1970s ushered in both a restructuring of the economy and a long-term decline in real wages and social benefits. The massive layoffs due to technological development and the flight of capital decimated entire communities and continue to pose a huge challenge to the labor movement. Urban centers with large African American and Latino communities have seen unemployment rates soar.

Not coincidentally, the overthrow of the socialist camp was followed in short order by the near elimination of the "social safety net" in the United States. Welfare, food stamps and other nutrition programs, housing assistance and other key services were wiped out or drastically reduced by the combined efforts of a Democratic White House and a Republican Congress in 1995 to 1996.

The monstrous growth of the prison system, largely devoid of any education or job-training programs, means that today more than two million people—disproportionately from oppressed communities—are "warehoused" in concentration camps for the poor. More than 7 million people are "in the system": behind bars or on parole or probation. The U.S. prison population is the world's largest. More than 3,000 prisoners are facing the racist and anti-worker death penalty.

Almost one in four African American men between the ages of 20 and 29 are "in the system," as compared to one in 10 Latino men and one in 16 white men.

In a state that falsely poses as the paragon of "democracy," political prisoners like Mumia Abu-Jamal, Leonard Peltier and the Cuban Five, to name just a few, have been sentenced to execution or life imprisonment. Torture has become commonplace, not only in the U.S.-administered prisons in Iraq and the U.S. naval base at Guantánamo Bay, Cuba, but in the prisons inside the United States as well.

The health care crisis is intensifying rapidly in the United States. The root cause is that health care services are treated as any other commodity under capitalism; they are produced by the health industry capitalists not primarily to meet human needs but for profit. The giant hospital, pharmaceutical, medical equipment and, especially, the powerful and parasitic insurance companies are reaping enormous profits from private health care. The huge mark-ups in the prices of health care goods and services have created a spiraling crisis and the deprivation of health benefits to tens of millions of people

Police violence targeting oppressed communities is an epidemic under capitalism.

PHOTO: REUTERS/ERIC THAYER

in the United States. Over the past five years, health care premiums have increased at three to four times the rate of inflation, between 10 to 15 percent annually.

HIV/AIDS drugs that can be produced for less than $300 cost up to $15,000 per year in the United States, because the big pharmaceutical monopolies are producing for profit and blocking the use of drugs produced by generic manufacturers in other countries. Though sub-Saharan Africa has just over 10 percent of the world's population, it is home to two-thirds of the people in the world who are infected with HIV and AIDS. Less than 1 percent of them have access to existing drugs.

In the United States, the HIV/AIDS epidemic is also a crisis, and today is the leading cause of death among African Americans between the ages of 35 and 44.

Capitalism's unquenchable thirst for profit has intensified the attacks on the environment. The "war on terrorism" and "homeland security" have been used to justify drastically lower air quality standards, opening up the Arctic and other areas for mineral and timber exploitation, and environmental racism—toxic and radioactive waste dumping in predominantly oppressed communities. Washington, acting on behalf of corporate polluters, has refused to sign even such a modest global warming agreement as the Kyoto Protocol.

These unprecedented attacks and intensified exploitation form the objective basis for a massive counter offensive led by the working class. The task facing all those who aspire to provide leadership to this counter offensive is developing the analysis, strategy and tactics to unleash the historic power of our class.

THE HISTORIC TASK OF UNITY

Since its inception, U.S. society has been marked by extreme racism. This has been the predominant obstacle to confronting the ruling-class offensive.

The struggle of those who have been most oppressed by the racist system has led to major legal, social and economic reforms. Nonetheless, pervasive racism remains a dominant fact of life. Youth from the Black, Latino and other nationally oppressed communities are confronted daily with police brutality and murder. They routinely face racist profiling in commercial establishments, as well as being shut out and "tracked" by racist practices in the educational system. The ruling-class assault on hard-won gains from past decades continues.

Affirmative action and equal education are under attack by the ruling class and its governments at federal and state levels. Affirmative action, which had barely begun to redress the gross inequalities suffered by oppressed nationalities and women, has been rolled back, gutted and repealed outright in many areas. A number of other gains that were won in the wake of the mass Civil Rights revolution of the 1950s and 1960s—like women's rights, lesbian/gay/bi/trans rights, equal marriage rights and disabled rights—are suffering a similar fate.

On the 56th anniversary of *Brown v. Board of Education* in 2010, the "separate and unequal" resegregation of public schools—never more than partially desegregated anyway—is notoriously widespread. For African American and other students of color attending integrated schools, patterns of racism impose an array of obstacles to achieving "equal education."

Public education for all working-class children and youth has been allowed to deteriorate to the extreme. For many students, especially African American, Latino, Native, Asian, Arab and working-class whites, the alternatives are the military, low-paid jobs or prison once their "education" is completed.

As an oppressed nation within the United States, the Black population continues to lag behind the majority white population in every social index. Black, Latino and other communities of color still occupy the most exploited segment of the working class, facing grinding poverty, unemployment and low wages compounded by racist violence and police-state terror.

The capitalist state has deepened the exploitation of immigrants by means of repressive legislation and denial of elementary rights. Mass roundups and deportations of undocumented immigrants are meant to terrorize, subjecting them to even more extreme exploitation. The aim is also to divide and weaken the working class and force down the wages of all workers.

The PSL defends the right of self-determination for oppressed nations within the United States. At the same time, we fight for the unity of the multinational working class against our common enemy, the racist capitalist class of bankers and corporate owners.

Women's continuing subordinate position in society, at home and on the job, originated in the rise of class society. It has been compounded today by cuts in welfare benefits, child care and health care as well as by racism. Women continue to be subjected to violence and exploitation in capitalist society.

Women's reproductive rights are under continued attack at the federal and state level. The huge April 2004 demonstration of more than 1 million women and their allies in Washington, D.C., in defense of women's right to choose—whatever its limitations in political orientation toward the Democratic Party and its limited mobilization of women of color—was a powerful demonstration of the power of a grassroots movement, the primary barrier to the rollback of women's rights.

Over the past three decades or more, there have been important partial gains toward equal rights achieved through mass struggle by the LGBT communities. Now, a fierce battle is raging over same-sex marriage and the entitlement of same-sex couples to equal rights and benefits.

As a member of the ANSWER Coalition, the PSL has helped mobilize hundreds of thousands of people against imperialist war.

The ruling-class resistance to extending basic civil marriage rights to same-sex couples is not based only on reactionary ideology. Even where domestic partnership exists, more than 1,000 rights and benefits extended to heterosexual couples are denied to same-sex partners. Denial of these same benefits means additional billions of dollars in profit for the capitalists, giving a material basis for reactionary anti-gay ideas.

A massive attack has been launched on civil rights and liberties. Immigrants have been hard hit, particularly immigrants from Arab and Muslim countries, through the USA Patriot Act and other legislation and executive orders. Torture, long-term imprisonment without charge or the right to legal counsel, secret court proceedings and more have been declared legal and acceptable by the highest government officials.

The U.S. working class continues to be stratified along economic lines and divided by racism, sexism, bigotry and national chauvinism. At the same time, the continually evolving character of capitalist technology is having dramatic and generally leveling effects on the working class. The working class is becoming more multinational and more integrated, at the same time as exploitation is intensifying, creating the conditions for a rise in class consciousness.

On every issue facing our class, the PSL stands among the most forceful fighters with the oppressed. Class unity is forged by the common struggles of our class, through which bigotry can be overcome.

In its short history, the PSL has given leadership to the struggle against U.S. imperialism, militarism and racism. As the anchoring organization in the ANSWER Coalition (Act Now to Stop War and End Racism), PSL members have taken the lead in organizing numerous mass national actions to stop the wars on Afghanistan and Iraq, mobilizing hundreds of thousands of people in the United States.

ANSWER has taken an unequivocal and explicit stand not only against U.S. wars, but also against imperialism and in support of the right of self-determination for all oppressed nations. Major campaigns against U.S.-backed wars on the Palestinian and Lebanese peoples have been initiated and led by ANSWER. At the same time, the ANSWER Coalition has sought to link together with the anti-war movement the fight against racism, immigrant bashing, sexism, anti-LGBT bigotry and all attacks on working people. This is just one important aspect of the PSL's ongoing work.

The PSL aims to build a militant, class-conscious working-class movement—independent of the capitalist parties—that fights for the interests of the working class on all issues.

At important points in history, unions have played a key role in advancing the fight for workers, organized and unorganized. Although the leadership of the AFL-CIO union federation has been

PHOTO: BETHANY MALMGREN

historically infected by racism, bureaucracy, chauvinism and ties to the government—especially since the anti-communist purges of the 1940s—labor strikes and protests have brought workers together in struggle across the many divides that are reinforced throughout capitalist society. In recent years, there has been a growing struggle inside the labor movement to oppose the Iraq war and to make the connection between militarism, war and capitalist globalization.

The struggle to simply maintain health care coverage has become the central issue in union negotiations and strikes across the United States. Union organizing, especially in the private sector, has been made more difficult than at any time since the early 1930s. The massive relocation of industry and manufacturing out of the United States or into more isolated rural and semi-rural areas, combined with anti-labor government policies, has had the effect of further reducing the percentage of unionized workers. Today, less than 13 percent of all employees in the United States are union members, the lowest percentage in 70 years.

The continued interconnections between top labor leaders and the imperialist state produce shameful class betrayals like aid to the corrupt and counterrevolutionary "labor leaders" in Venezuela; refusal to recognize the connection between the war budget and economic attacks on workers; silence on the Iraq war; and unconditional support for Israel. This relationship also hamstrings the labor movement as a progressive force in U.S. society. The labor leadership has subordinated itself to the Democratic Party.

Yet unions remain the most numerous and powerful organizations of the working class. They must be renewed and strengthened for the struggle to go forward. □

Part 4

The need for a revolutionary party

WE recognize that there is a dialectical relationship between the struggle—that is, the movement of people for change—and political consciousness. Without mass struggle, there is no hope for real change. But activism alone is not enough to develop a class-conscious socialist movement. That requires the intervention of a revolutionary Marxist party.

A mass revolutionary workers party is necessary for the achievement of socialism. Unlike the bourgeoisie when it was a rising but still oppressed class in Europe under feudalism, the working class is not accumulating ever increasing wealth in its hands.

The spontaneous accumulation of wealth in the form of capital made the eventual triumph of the capitalist class inevitable. But, as Marx showed, the working class is continually growing poorer in relation to its class enemy. That is due to the process of extracting surplus value—not paying the workers for the full value of the goods and services that they produce—which is the foundation of capitalist wealth.

The great advantages of the working class are its ever growing numbers and its strategic position in society. Yet, these advantages remain only potential strengths unless the working class is conscious and organized. Today the very numerous and diverse U.S. working class is largely atomized and unorganized.

A revolution cannot take place without society entering into a revolutionary crisis, a crisis that shakes the foundations of bourgeois rule and makes a large section of the masses refuse to go on living in the old way. A revolution is a life-and-death battle.

As many experiences have shown over the past century, the opportunity to carry out a successful revolution usually lasts for only a short time. The results of moving forward either too early or too late can be disastrous for the entire working class. The party cannot sub-stitute itself for the masses; it must win their confidence by showing that it can provide the strategy and tactics necessary for victory.

How and when a revolutionary crisis comes about is entirely unpredictable and outside the control of either revolutionaries or the ruling class. Most often in the last century it has been a byproduct of war. What revolutionaries do have some control over is not when or how a new crisis will develop, but what type of organization will be available when a revolutionary crisis does arise, as it inevitably will. How strong, multinational, experienced, widespread, numerous and united will the revolutionary party be? How steeled will it be in many and widely varying struggles? How has it measured up to challenges, especially in earlier times of crisis?

To the question of what revolutionaries do in non-revolutionary times, Lenin's answer was clear: Build the party, build the organization without which the revolutionary opportunity cannot be transformed into a revolutionary victory. Build now, because if you wait, it will be too late. From Lenin's point of view, the entire reason for the party from the very beginning was preparation for the revolutionary opportunity.

Preparation means many things. It means studying and absorb-ing the lessons of past movements and revolutions. It means being involved in the most critical struggles of the day, at the points of greatest conflict between the classes. It means fighting to win the movements that respond spontaneously to smaller crises in capitalist society to a truly progressive and revolutionary outlook.

It means organizing the party itself for the multiplicity of chal-lenges that it faces. It means a commitment to recruiting new cadre from among the many new and not so new activists, particularly among the most exploited and oppressed workers. The structure and operating principles of the party are based on democratic centralism: internal democratic debate combined with unity in action. Success in confronting the bureaucratically and militarily centralized capital-ist state is inconceivable without a centralized working-class party and movement.

Deep involvement in the struggle against racism is the duty of a workers' party, and critical for the building of working-class unity. The forging of multinational unity among the U.S. working class is also won in the struggle.

History shows that it is the living struggle to overcome class oppression that educates workers on the need for unity and opposition to racism, in order to win. The role of a party and its members is to help advance those struggles and provide clarity on the root cause of class and national oppression, the capitalist system itself.

For a revolutionary working-class party, organization is not an end in itself. The party seeks to unite the most advanced sectors in the working-class movement in preparation for a larger struggle. In the day-in, day-out struggle against every manifestation of imperialist war and capitalist oppression, the party must become the center of action. It must seek the theoretical, political and organizational collaboration of the most advanced groups that are engaged in struggle.

It will be through the practical struggle—with all of its attendant theoretical and political questions—that the greatest unity can be achieved among those who form and continually replenish the ranks of revolutionary cadres. A top priority must be to create a structure that advances the struggles of workers, especially the sections of the working class who suffer the greatest oppression and who, as a consequence, will be the best fighters and leaders in the movement against imperialism and capitalism.

The Party for Socialism and Liberation is dedicated to building a new revolutionary workers' party in the heartland of world imperialism. We need the participation of organizers and activists from all over the country. Whether you have ever been involved before or not, we invite all those who share our viewpoint to join us. Together, we can win! □

Contact the Party for Socialism and Liberation

NATIONAL OFFICES

San Francisco, CA
sf@pslweb.org
3181 Mission St., #13
San Francisco, CA 94110
415-821-6171

Washington, DC
dc@pslweb.org
PO Box 26451
Washington, DC 20001
202-234-2828

BRANCHES

Albuquerque, NM
abq@pslweb.org
505-503-3067

Austin, TX
austin@pslweb.org
512-577-4749

Baltimore MD
baltimore@pslweb.org
443-378-925

Boston, MA
boston@pslweb.org

Chicago, IL
chicago@pslweb.org
773-920-7590

Long Beach, CA
lb@pslweb.org

Los Angeles, CA
la@pslweb.org
323-810-3380

Miami, FL
miami@pslweb.org
305-710-3189

New Haven, CT
ct@pslweb.org
203-416-8365

New Paltz, NY
np@pslweb.org

New York City, NY
nyc@pslweb.org
212-694-8762

Philadelphia, PA
philly@pslweb.org

San Diego CA
sandiego@pslweb.org

San Jose, CA
sanjose@pslweb.org
408-829-9507

Seattle, WA
seattle@pslweb.org
206-367-3820

Sioux Falls, SD
sodak@pslweb.org

Syracuse, NY
syracuse@pslweb.org

for a complete listing visit PSLweb.org